HAL•LEONARD

JAZZ PLAY-ALONG®

Book and CD for B♭, E♭, C and Bass Clef Instruments

VOLUME 145

Arranged and Produced by
Mark Taylor

Country STANDARDS

<table>
<tr><td rowspan="2">**TITLE**</td><td colspan="4">**PAGE NUMBERS**</td></tr>
<tr><td>C Treble
Instruments</td><td>B♭
Instruments</td><td>E♭
Instruments</td><td>C Bass
Instruments</td></tr>
<tr><td>Always on My Mind</td><td>4</td><td>22</td><td>40</td><td>58</td></tr>
<tr><td>Crazy</td><td>6</td><td>24</td><td>42</td><td>60</td></tr>
<tr><td>I Will Always Love You</td><td>8</td><td>26</td><td>44</td><td>62</td></tr>
<tr><td>Lookin' for Love</td><td>10</td><td>28</td><td>46</td><td>64</td></tr>
<tr><td>Night Life</td><td>12</td><td>30</td><td>48</td><td>66</td></tr>
<tr><td>On the Road Again</td><td>14</td><td>32</td><td>50</td><td>68</td></tr>
<tr><td>Tennessee Waltz</td><td>16</td><td>34</td><td>52</td><td>70</td></tr>
<tr><td>To All the Girls I've Loved Before</td><td>18</td><td>36</td><td>54</td><td>72</td></tr>
<tr><td>Wichita Lineman</td><td>20</td><td>38</td><td>56</td><td>74</td></tr>
<tr><td>You Are My Sunshine</td><td>5</td><td>23</td><td>41</td><td>59</td></tr>
</table>

<table>
<tr><td>**TITLE**</td><td>CD Track Number
Split Track/Melody</td><td>CD Track Number
Full Stereo Track</td></tr>
<tr><td>Always on My Mind</td><td>1</td><td>2</td></tr>
<tr><td>Crazy</td><td>3</td><td>4</td></tr>
<tr><td>I Will Always Love You</td><td>5</td><td>6</td></tr>
<tr><td>Lookin' for Love</td><td>7</td><td>8</td></tr>
<tr><td>Night Life</td><td>9</td><td>10</td></tr>
<tr><td>On the Road Again</td><td>11</td><td>12</td></tr>
<tr><td>Tennessee Waltz</td><td>13</td><td>14</td></tr>
<tr><td>To All the Girls I've Loved Before</td><td>15</td><td>16</td></tr>
<tr><td>Wichita Lineman</td><td>17</td><td>18</td></tr>
<tr><td>You Are My Sunshine</td><td>19</td><td>20</td></tr>
<tr><td>B♭ Tuning Notes</td><td></td><td>21</td></tr>
</table>

ISBN 978-1-4584-1646-9

HAL•LEONARD®
CORPORATION

7777 W. BLUEMOUND RD. P.O. BOX 13819 MILWAUKEE, WI 53213

T0050726

Visit Hal Leonard Online at
www.halleonard.com

COUNTRY STANDARDS

Volume 145

Arranged and Produced by
Mark Taylor

Featured Players:

Graham Breedlove–Trumpet
John Desalme–Tenor Sax
Tony Nalker–Piano
Regan Brough–Bass
Todd Harrison–Drums

Recorded at Bias Studios, Springfield, Virginia
Bob Dawson, Engineer

HOW TO USE THE CD:

Each song has <u>two</u> tracks:

1) Split Track/Melody

Woodwind, **Brass**, **Keyboard**, and **Mallet Players** can use this track as a learning tool for melody style and inflection.

Bass Players can learn and perform with this track – remove the recorded bass track by turning down the volume on the LEFT channel.

Keyboard and **Guitar Players** can learn and perform with this track – remove the recorded piano part by turning down the volume on the RIGHT channel.

2) Full Stereo Track

Soloists or **Groups** can learn and perform with this accompaniment track with the RHYTHM SECTION only.

CD

① : SPLIT TRACK/MELODY
② : FULL STEREO TRACK

ALWAYS ON MY MIND

WORDS AND MUSIC BY WAYNE THOMPSON,
MARK JAMES AND JOHNNY CHRISTOPHER

C VERSION

YOU ARE MY SUNSHINE

CD
19 : SPLIT TRACK/MELODY
20 : FULL STEREO TRACK

WORDS AND MUSIC BY
JIMMIE DAVIS

CD

◆3 : SPLIT TRACK/MELODY
◆4 : FULL STEREO TRACK

CRAZY

WORDS AND MUSIC BY
WILLIE NELSON

C VERSION

MEDIUM SLOW COUNTRY BALLAD

I WILL ALWAYS LOVE YOU

WORDS AND MUSIC BY
DOLLY PARTON

C VERSION

Lookin' For Love

FROM URBAN COWBOY

WORDS AND MUSIC BY WANDA MALLETTE,
PATTI RYAN AND BOB MORRISON

C VERSION

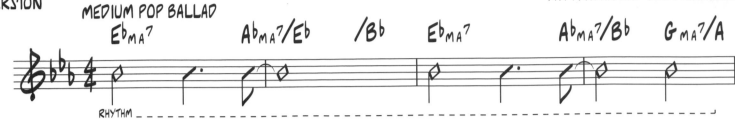

CD

◆ 9 : SPLIT TRACK/MELODY
◆ 10 : FULL STEREO TRACK

C VERSION

NIGHT LIFE

WORDS AND MUSIC BY WILLIE NELSON,
WALT BREELAND AND PAUL BUSKIRK

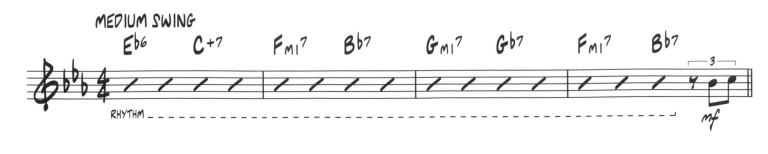

ON THE ROAD AGAIN

WORDS AND MUSIC BY
WILLIE NELSON

C VERSION

TENNESSEE WALTZ

WORDS AND MUSIC BY REDD STEWART
AND PEE WEE KING

C VERSION

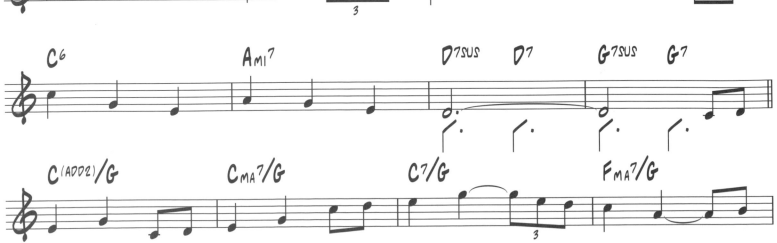

15 : SPLIT TRACK/MELODY
16 : FULL STEREO TRACK

TO ALL THE GIRLS I'VE LOVED BEFORE

LYRIC BY HAL DAVID
MUSIC BY ALBERT HAMMOND

C VERSION

WICHITA LINEMAN

CD
◆17 : SPLIT TRACK/MELODY
◆18 : FULL STEREO TRACK

WORDS AND MUSIC BY
JIMMY WEBB

C VERSION

BRIGHT JAZZ WALTZ

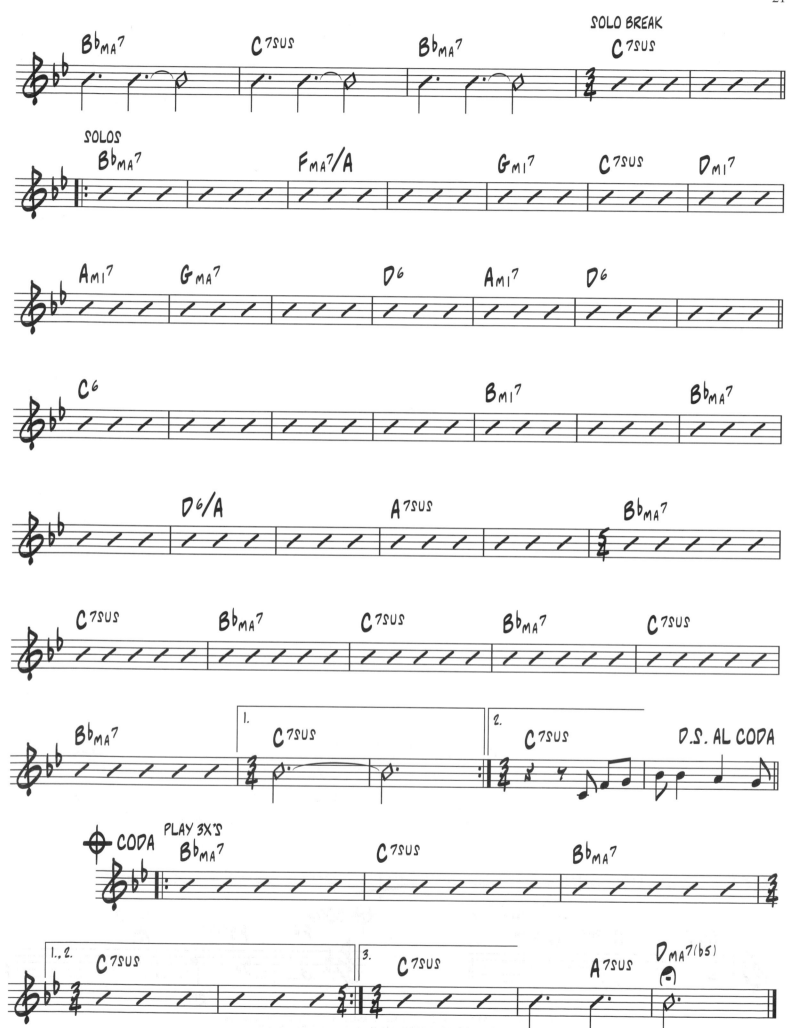

Always on My Mind

WORDS AND MUSIC BY WAYNE THOMPSON, MARK JAMES AND JOHNNY CHRISTOPHER

YOU ARE MY SUNSHINE

WORDS AND MUSIC BY
JIMMIE DAVIS

Bb VERSION

CRAZY

WORDS AND MUSIC BY
WILLIE NELSON

Bb VERSION

I WILL ALWAYS LOVE YOU

WORDS AND MUSIC BY
DOLLY PARTON

Bb VERSION

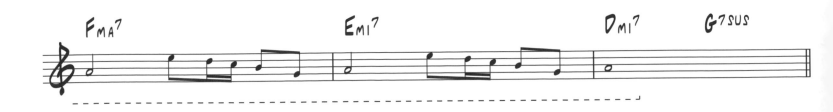

Lookin' For Love

FROM URBAN COWBOY

WORDS AND MUSIC BY WANDA MALLETTE,
PATTI RYAN AND BOB MORRISON

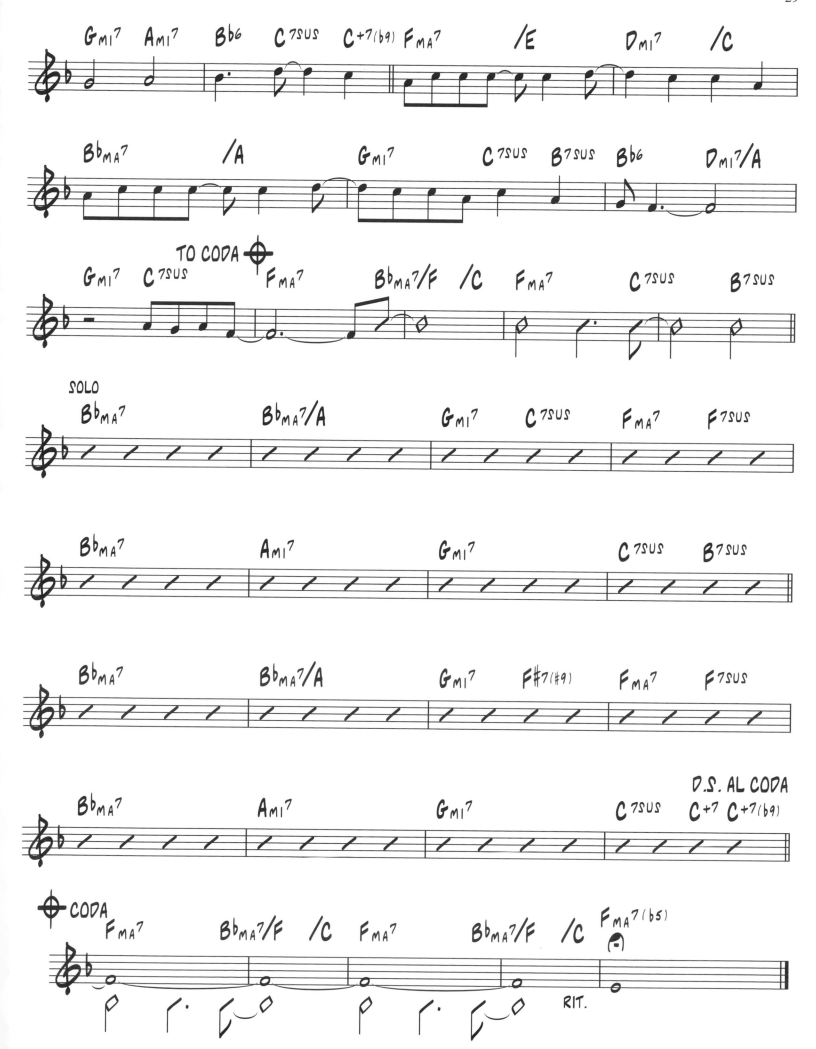

NIGHT LIFE

WORDS AND MUSIC BY WILLIE NELSON,
WALT BREELAND AND PAUL BUSKIRK

CD
9 : SPLIT TRACK/MELODY
10 : FULL STEREO TRACK

Bb VERSION

ON THE ROAD AGAIN

WORDS AND MUSIC BY
WILLIE NELSON

Tennessee Waltz

WORDS AND MUSIC BY REDD STEWART
AND PEE WEE KING

Bb VERSION

TO ALL THE GIRLS I'VE LOVED BEFORE

15 : SPLIT TRACK/MELODY
16 : FULL STEREO TRACK

LYRIC BY HAL DAVID
MUSIC BY ALBERT HAMMOND

Bb VERSION

WICHITA LINEMAN

WORDS AND MUSIC BY
JIMMY WEBB

CD
⬥**17** : SPLIT TRACK/MELODY
⬥**18** : FULL STEREO TRACK

Bb VERSION

BRIGHT JAZZ WALTZ

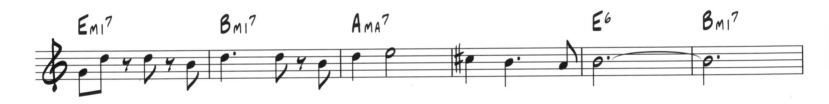

TO CODA ⊕

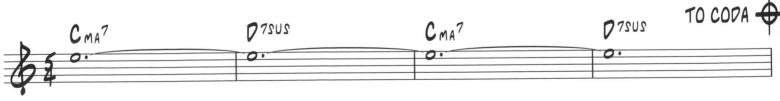

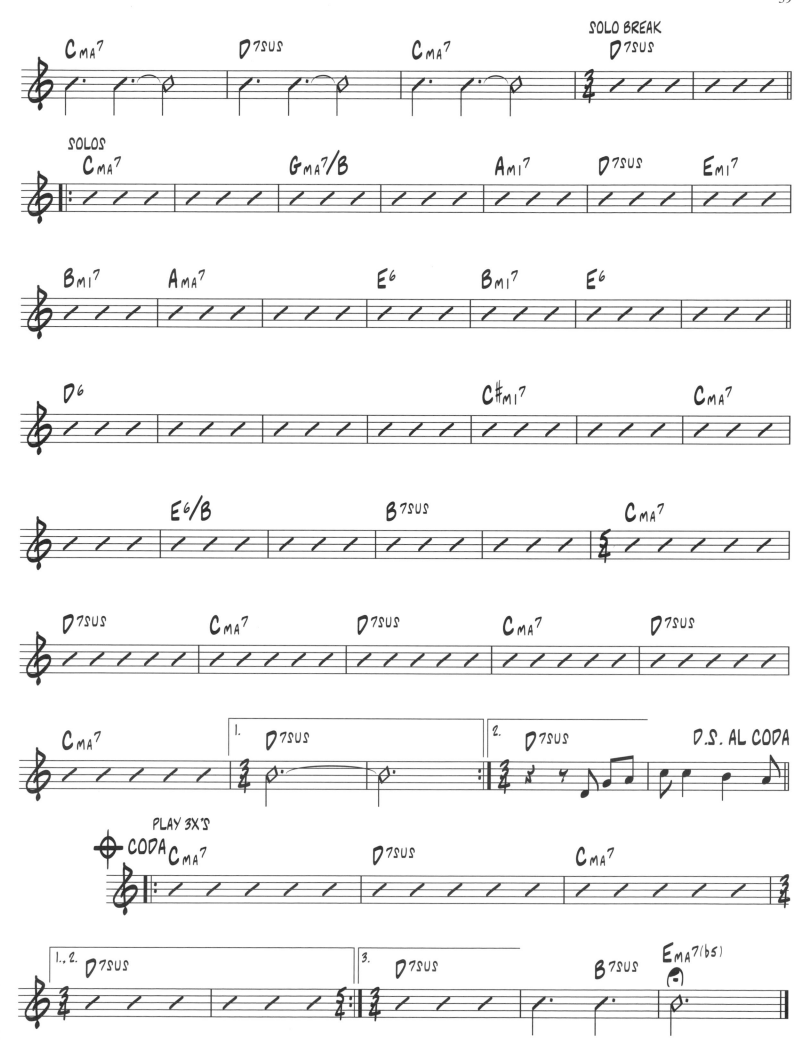

Always on My Mind

WORDS AND MUSIC BY WAYNE THOMPSON,
MARK JAMES AND JOHNNY CHRISTOPHER

Eb VERSION

YOU ARE MY SUNSHINE

WORDS AND MUSIC BY
JIMMIE DAVIS

CRAZY

WORDS AND MUSIC BY
WILLIE NELSON

CD
❸ : SPLIT TRACK/MELODY
❹ : FULL STEREO TRACK

Eb VERSION

I WILL ALWAYS LOVE YOU

WORDS AND MUSIC BY
DOLLY PARTON

Eb VERSION

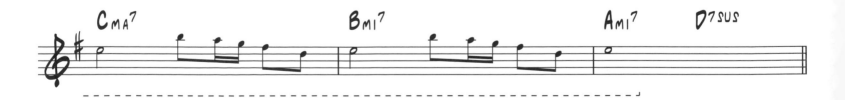

Lookin' For Love

FROM URBAN COWBOY

WORDS AND MUSIC BY WANDA MALLETTE, PATTI RYAN AND BOB MORRISON

Night Life

Eb VERSION

WORDS AND MUSIC BY WILLIE NELSON,
WALT BREELAND AND PAUL BUSKIRK

49

ON THE ROAD AGAIN

WORDS AND MUSIC BY
WILLIE NELSON

TENNESSEE WALTZ

WORDS AND MUSIC BY REDD STEWART
AND PEE WEE KING

CD
13: SPLIT TRACK/MELODY
14: FULL STEREO TRACK

Eb VERSION

MEDIUM SLOW JAZZ WALTZ

TO ALL THE GIRLS I'VE LOVED BEFORE

LYRIC BY HAL DAVID
MUSIC BY ALBERT HAMMOND

Eb VERSION

WICHITA LINEMAN

WORDS AND MUSIC BY
JIMMY WEBB

CD
17 : SPLIT TRACK/MELODY
18 : FULL STEREO TRACK

Eb VERSION

BRIGHT JAZZ WALTZ

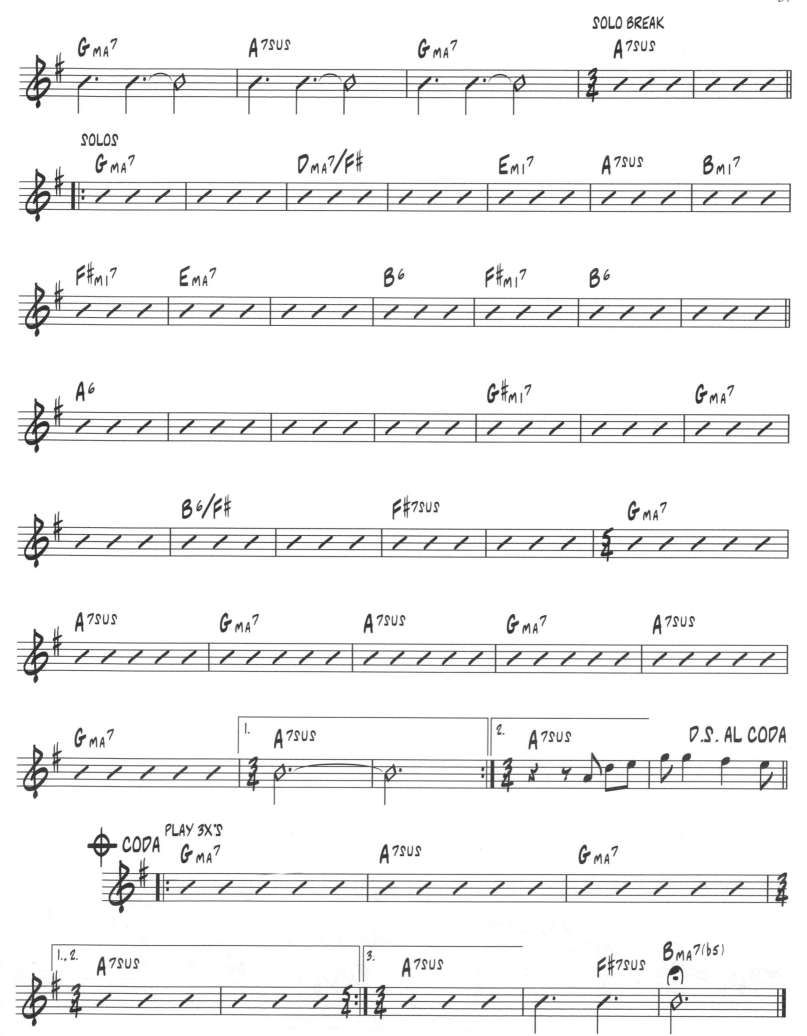

Always On My Mind

WORDS AND MUSIC BY WAYNE THOMPSON,
MARK JAMES AND JOHNNY CHRISTOPHER

YOU ARE MY SUNSHINE

WORDS AND MUSIC BY
JIMMIE DAVIS

CRAZY

WORDS AND MUSIC BY
WILLIE NELSON

I WILL ALWAYS LOVE YOU

WORDS AND MUSIC BY
DOLLY PARTON

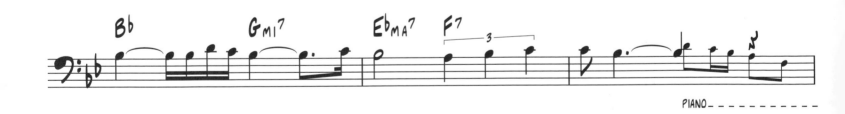

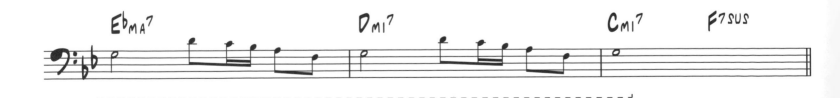

CD

: SPLIT TRACK/MELODY

: FULL STEREO TRACK

𝄢: C VERSION

Lookin' For Love

FROM URBAN COWBOY

WORDS AND MUSIC BY WANDA MALLETTE,
PATTI RYAN AND BOB MORRISON

NIGHT LIFE

WORDS AND MUSIC BY WILLIE NELSON,
WALT BREELAND AND PAUL BUSKIRK

ON THE ROAD AGAIN

WORDS AND MUSIC BY
WILLIE NELSON

Tennessee Waltz

WORDS AND MUSIC BY REDD STEWART
AND PEE WEE KING

TO ALL THE GIRLS I'VE LOVED BEFORE

LYRIC BY HAL DAVID
MUSIC BY ALBERT HAMMOND

WICHITA LINEMAN

WORDS AND MUSIC BY
JIMMY WEBB

Presenting the Hal Leonard JAZZ PLAY-ALONG SERIES

For use with all B-flat, E-flat, Bass Clef and C instruments, the Jazz Play-Along® Series is the ultimate learning tool for all jazz musicians. With musician-friendly lead sheets, melody cues, and other split-track choices on the included CD, these first-of-a-kind packages help you master improvisation while playing some of the greatest tunes of all time. FOR STUDY, each tune includes a split track with: melody cue with proper style and inflection • professional rhythm tracks • choruses for soloing • removable bass part • removable piano part. FOR PERFORMANCE, each tune also has: an additional full stereo accompaniment track (no melody) • additional choruses for soloing.

1A. MAIDEN VOYAGE/ALL BLUES
00843158 .... $15.99

1. DUKE ELLINGTON
00841644 .... $16.95

2. MILES DAVIS
00841645 .... $16.95

3. THE BLUES
00841646 .... $16.99

4. JAZZ BALLADS
00841691 .... $16.99

5. BEST OF BEBOP
00841689 .... $16.95

6. JAZZ CLASSICS WITH EASY CHANGES
00841690 .... $16.99

7. ESSENTIAL JAZZ STANDARDS
00843000 .... $16.99

8. ANTONIO CARLOS JOBIM AND THE ART OF THE BOSSA NOVA
00843001 .... $16.95

9. DIZZY GILLESPIE
00843002 .... $16.99

10. DISNEY CLASSICS
00843003 .... $16.99

11. RODGERS AND HART FAVORITES
00843004 .... $16.99

12. ESSENTIAL JAZZ CLASSICS
00843005 .... $16.99

13. JOHN COLTRANE
00843006 .... $16.95

14. IRVING BERLIN
00843007 .... $15.99

15. RODGERS & HAMMERSTEIN
00843008 .... $15.99

16. COLE PORTER
00843009 .... $15.95

17. COUNT BASIE
00843010 .... $16.95

18. HAROLD ARLEN
00843011 .... $15.95

19. COOL JAZZ
00843012 .... $15.95

20. CHRISTMAS CAROLS
00843080 .... $14.95

21. RODGERS AND HART CLASSICS
00843014 .... $14.95

22. WAYNE SHORTER
00843015 .... $16.95

23. LATIN JAZZ
00843016 .... $16.95

24. EARLY JAZZ STANDARDS
00843017 .... $14.95

25. CHRISTMAS JAZZ
00843018 .... $16.95

26. CHARLIE PARKER
00843019 .... $16.95

27. GREAT JAZZ STANDARDS
00843020 .... $16.99

28. BIG BAND ERA
00843021 .... $15.99

29. LENNON AND MCCARTNEY
00843022 .... $16.95

30. BLUES' BEST
00843023 .... $15.99

31. JAZZ IN THREE
00843024 .... $15.99

32. BEST OF SWING
00843025 .... $15.99

33. SONNY ROLLINS
00843029 .... $15.95

34. ALL TIME STANDARDS
00843030 .... $15.99

35. BLUESY JAZZ
00843031 .... $16.99

36. HORACE SILVER
00843032 .... $16.99

37. BILL EVANS
00843033 .... $16.95

38. YULETIDE JAZZ
00843034 .... $16.95

39. "ALL THE THINGS YOU ARE" & MORE JEROME KERN SONGS
00843035 .... $15.99

40. BOSSA NOVA
00843036 .... $16.99

41. CLASSIC DUKE ELLINGTON
00843037 .... $16.99

42. GERRY MULLIGAN FAVORITES
00843038 .... $16.99

43. GERRY MULLIGAN CLASSICS
00843039 .... $16.99

44. OLIVER NELSON
00843040 .... $16.95

45. JAZZ AT THE MOVIES
00843041 .... $15.99

46. BROADWAY JAZZ STANDARDS
00843042 .... $15.99

47. CLASSIC JAZZ BALLADS
00843043 .... $15.99

48. BEBOP CLASSICS
00843044 .... $16.99

49. MILES DAVIS STANDARDS
00843045 .... $16.95

50. GREAT JAZZ CLASSICS
00843046 .... $15.99

51. UP-TEMPO JAZZ
00843047 .... $15.99

52. STEVIE WONDER
00843048 .... $16.99

53. RHYTHM CHANGES
00843049 .... $15.99

54. "MOONLIGHT IN VERMONT" AND OTHER GREAT STANDARDS
00843050 .... $15.99

55. BENNY GOLSON
00843052 .... $15.95

56. "GEORGIA ON MY MIND" & OTHER SONGS BY HOAGY CARMICHAEL
00843056 .... $15.99

57. VINCE GUARALDI
00843057 .... $16.99

58. MORE LENNON AND MCCARTNEY
00843059 .... $16.99

59. SOUL JAZZ
00843060 .... $16.99

60. DEXTER GORDON
00843061 .... $15.95

61. MONGO SANTAMARIA
00843062 .... $15.95

62. JAZZ-ROCK FUSION
00843063 .... $16.99

63. CLASSICAL JAZZ
00843064 .... $14.95

64. TV TUNES
00843065 .... $14.95

65. SMOOTH JAZZ
00843066 .... $16.99

66. A CHARLIE BROWN CHRISTMAS
00843067 .... $16.99

67. CHICK COREA
00843068 .... $15.95

68. CHARLES MINGUS
00843069 .... $16.95

69. CLASSIC JAZZ
00843071 .... $15.99

70. THE DOORS
00843072 .... $14.95

71. COLE PORTER CLASSICS
00843073 .... $14.95

72. CLASSIC JAZZ BALLADS
00843074 .... $15.99

73. JAZZ/BLUES
00843075 .... $14.95

74. BEST JAZZ CLASSICS
00843076 .... $15.99

75. PAUL DESMOND
00843077 .... $15.99

76. BROADWAY JAZZ BALLADS
00843078 .... $15.99

77. JAZZ ON BROADWAY
00843079 .... $15.99

78. STEELY DAN
00843070 .... $15.99

79. MILES DAVIS CLASSICS
00843081 .... $15.99

80. JIMI HENDRIX
00843083 .... $16.99

81. FRANK SINATRA – CLASSICS
00843084 .... $15.99

82. FRANK SINATRA – STANDARDS
00843085 .... $15.99

83. ANDREW LLOYD WEBBER
00843104 .... $14.95

84. BOSSA NOVA CLASSICS
00843105 .... $14.95

85. MOTOWN HITS
00843109 .... $14.95

86. BENNY GOODMAN
00843110 .... $15.99

87. DIXIELAND
00843111 .... $14.95

88. DUKE ELLINGTON FAVORITES
00843112 .... $14.95

89. IRVING BERLIN FAVORITES
00843113 .... $14.95

90. THELONIOUS MONK CLASSICS
00841262 .... $16.99

91. THELONIOUS MONK FAVORITES
00841263 .... $16.99

92. LEONARD BERNSTEIN
00450134 .... $15.99

93. DISNEY FAVORITES
00843142 .... $14.99

94. RAY
00843143 .... $14.99

95. JAZZ AT THE LOUNGE
00843144 .... $14.99

96. LATIN JAZZ STANDARDS
00843145 .... $15.99

97. MAYBE I'M AMAZED*
00843148 .... $15.99

98. DAVE FRISHBERG
00843149 .... $15.99

99. SWINGING STANDARDS
00843150 .... $14.99

100. LOUIS ARMSTRONG
00740423 .... $16.99

101. BUD POWELL
00843152 .... $14.99

102. JAZZ POP
00843153 .... $14.99

**103. ON GREEN DOLPHIN STREET
& OTHER JAZZ CLASSICS**
00843154 .... $14.99

104. ELTON JOHN
00843155 .... $14.99

105. SOULFUL JAZZ
00843151 .... $15.99

106. SLO' JAZZ
00843117 .... $14.99

107. MOTOWN CLASSICS
00843116 .... $14.99

108. JAZZ WALTZ
00843159 .... $15.99

109. OSCAR PETERSON
00843160 .... $16.99

110. JUST STANDARDS
00843161 .... $15.99

111. COOL CHRISTMAS
00843162 .... $15.99

112. PAQUITO D'RIVERA – LATIN JAZZ*
48020662 .... $16.99

113. PAQUITO D'RIVERA – BRAZILIAN JAZZ*
48020663 .... $19.99

114. MODERN JAZZ QUARTET FAVORITES
00843163 .... $15.99

115. THE SOUND OF MUSIC
00843164 .... $15.99

116. JACO PASTORIUS
00843165 .... $15.99

117. ANTONIO CARLOS JOBIM – MORE HITS
00843166 .... $15.99

118. BIG JAZZ STANDARDS COLLECTION
00843167 .... $27.50

119. JELLY ROLL MORTON
00843168 .... $15.99

120. J.S. BACH
00843169 .... $15.99

121. DJANGO REINHARDT
00843170 .... $15.99

122. PAUL SIMON
00843182 .... $16.99

123. BACHARACH & DAVID
00843185 .... $15.99

124. JAZZ-ROCK HORN HITS
00843186 .... $15.99

126. COUNT BASIE CLASSICS
00843157 .... $15.99

127. CHUCK MANGIONE
00843188 .... $15.99

128. VOCAL STANDARDS (LOW VOICE)
00843189 .... $15.99

129. VOCAL STANDARDS (HIGH VOICE)
00843190 .... $15.99

130. VOCAL JAZZ (LOW VOICE)
00843191 .... $15.99

131. VOCAL JAZZ (HIGH VOICE)
00843192 .... $15.99

132. STAN GETZ ESSENTIALS
00843193 .... $15.99

133. STAN GETZ FAVORITES
00843194 .... $15.99

134. NURSERY RHYMES*
00843196 .... $17.99

135. JEFF BECK
00843197 .... $15.99

136. NAT ADDERLEY
00843198 .... $15.99

137. WES MONTGOMERY
00843199 .... $15.99

138. FREDDIE HUBBARD
00843200 .... $15.99

139. JULIAN "CANNONBALL" ADDERLEY
00843201 .... $15.99

140. JOE ZAWINUL
00843202 .... $15.99

141. BILL EVANS STANDARDS
00843156 .... $15.99

142. CHARLIE PARKER GEMS
00843222 .... $15.99

150. JAZZ IMPROV BASICS
00843195 .... $19.99

151. MODERN JAZZ QUARTET CLASSICS
00843209 .... $15.99

152. J.J. JOHNSON
00843210 .... $15.99

154. HENRY MANCINI
00843213 .... $14.99

155. SMOOTH JAZZ CLASSICS
00843215 .... $15.99

156. THELONIOUS MONK – EARLY GEMS
00843216 .... $15.99

157. HYMNS
00843217 .... $15.99

158. JAZZ COVERS ROCK
00843219 .... $15.99

159. MOZART
00843220 .... $15.99

162. BIG CHRISTMAS COLLECTION
00843221 .... $24.99

*These CDs do not include split tracks.

Jazz Instruction & Improvisation
Books for All Instruments from Hal Leonard

AN APPROACH TO JAZZ IMPROVISATION
by Dave Pozzi
Musicians Institute Press

 INCLUDES TAB

Explore the styles of Charlie Parker, Sonny Rollins, Bud Powell and others with this comprehensive guide to jazz improvisation. Covers: scale choices • chord analysis • phrasing • melodies • harmonic progressions • more.
00695135 Book/CD Pack $17.95

BUILDING A JAZZ VOCABULARY
By Mike Steinel

A valuable resource for learning the basics of jazz from Mike Steinel of the University of North Texas. It covers: the basics of jazz • how to build effective solos • a comprehensive practice routine • and a jazz vocabulary of the masters.
00849911 ....$19.95

THE CYCLE OF FIFTHS
by Emile and Laura De Cosmo

This essential instruction book provides more than 450 exercises, including hundreds of melodic and rhythmic ideas. The book is designed to help improvisors master the cycle of fifths, one of the primary progressions in music. Guaranteed to refine technique, enhance improvisational fluency, and improve sight-reading!
00311114 ....$16.99

THE DIATONIC CYCLE
by Emile and Laura De Cosmo

Renowned jazz educators Emile and Laura De Cosmo provide more than 300 exercises to help improvisors tackle one of music's most common progressions: the diatonic cycle. This book is guaranteed to refine technique, enhance improvisational fluency, and improve sight-reading!
00311115 ....$16.95

 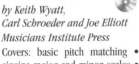

EAR TRAINING
by Keith Wyatt,
Carl Schroeder and Joe Elliott
Musicians Institute Press

Covers: basic pitch matching • singing major and minor scales • identifying intervals • transcribing melodies and rhythm • identifying chords and progressions • seventh chords and the blues • modal interchange, chromaticism, modulation • and more.
00695198 Book/2-CD Pack......................$24.95

EXERCISES AND ETUDES FOR THE JAZZ INSTRUMENTALIST
by J.J. Johnson

Designed as study material and playable by any instrument, these pieces run the gamut of the jazz experience, featuring common and uncommon time signatures and keys, and styles from ballads to funk. They are progressively graded so that both beginners and professionals will be challenged by the demands of this wonderful music.
00842018 Bass Clef Edition....................$16.95
00842042 Treble Clef Edition $16.95

JAZZOLOGY
THE ENCYCLOPEDIA OF JAZZ THEORY FOR ALL MUSICIANS
by Robert Rawlins and Nor Eddine Bahha

This comprehensive resource covers a variety of jazz topics, for beginners and pros of any instrument. The book serves as an encyclopedia for reference, a thorough methodology for the student, and a workbook for the classroom.
00311167 ....$19.99

JAZZ JAM SESSION
15 TRACKS INCLUDING RHYTHM CHANGES, BLUES, BOSSA, BALLADS & MORE
by Ed Friedland

Bring your local jazz jam session home! These essential jazz rhythm grooves feature a professional rhythm section and are perfect for guitar, harmonica, keyboard, saxophone and trumpet players to hone their soloing skills. The feels, tempos and keys have been varied to broaden your jazz experience. Styles include: ballads, bebop, blues, bossa nova, cool jazz, and more, with improv guidelines for each track.
00311827 Book/CD Pack $19.99

JAZZ THEORY RESOURCES
by Bert Ligon
Houston Publishing, Inc.

This is a jazz theory text in two volumes. **Volume 1 includes:** review of basic theory • rhythm in jazz performance • triadic generalization • diatonic harmonic progressions and analysis • substitutions and turnarounds • and more. **Volume 2 includes:** modes and modal frameworks • quartal harmony • extended tertian structures and triadic superimposition • pentatonic applications • coloring "outside" the lines and beyond • and more.
00030458 Volume 1 ....$39.95
00030459 Volume 2 ....$29.95

Prices, contents & availability subject to change without notice.

JOY OF IMPROV
by Dave Frank and John Amaral

This book/CD course on improvisation for all instruments and all styles will help players develop monster musical skills! **Book One** imparts a solid basis in technique, rhythm, chord theory, ear training and improv concepts. **Book Two** explores more advanced chord voicings, chord arranging techniques and more challenging blues and melodic lines. The CD can be used as a listening and play-along tool.
00220005 Book 1 – Book/CD Pack $27.99
00220006 Book 2 – Book/CD Pack $24.95

THE PATH TO JAZZ IMPROVISATION
by Emile and Laura De Cosmo

This fascinating jazz instruction book offers an innovative, scholarly approach to the art of improvisation. It includes in-depth analysis and lessons about: cycle of fifths • diatonic cycle • overtone series • pentatonic scale • harmonic and melodic minor scale • polytonal order of keys • blues and bebop scales • modes • and more.
00310904 ....$14.95

THE SOURCE
THE DICTIONARY OF CONTEMPORARY AND TRADITIONAL SCALES
by Steve Barta

This book serves as an informative guide for people who are looking for good, solid information regarding scales, chords, and how they work together. It provides right and left hand fingerings for scales, chords, and complete inversions. Includes over 20 different scales, each written in all 12 keys.
00240885 ....$17.99

21 BEBOP EXERCISES
by Steve Rawlins

This book/CD pack is both a warm-up collection and a manual for bebop phrasing. Its tasty and sophisticated exercises will help you develop your proficiency with jazz interpretation. It concentrates on practice in all twelve keys – moving higher by half-step – to help develop dexterity and range. The companion CD includes all of the exercises in 12 keys.
00315341 Book/CD Pack $17.95

FOR MORE INFORMATION, SEE YOUR LOCAL MUSIC DEALER, OR WRITE TO:

HAL•LEONARD® CORPORATION
7777 W. BLUEMOUND RD. P.O. BOX 13819 MILWAUKEE, WI 53213

Visit Hal Leonard online at
www.halleonard.com

0911